The New H

Bob Seberry

Senior Lecturer in Technology & Science
Education in Primary Schools at
Homerton College

Sheila Mallinson

Primary School teacher, Cambridge

Illustrated by
Jan Nesbitt

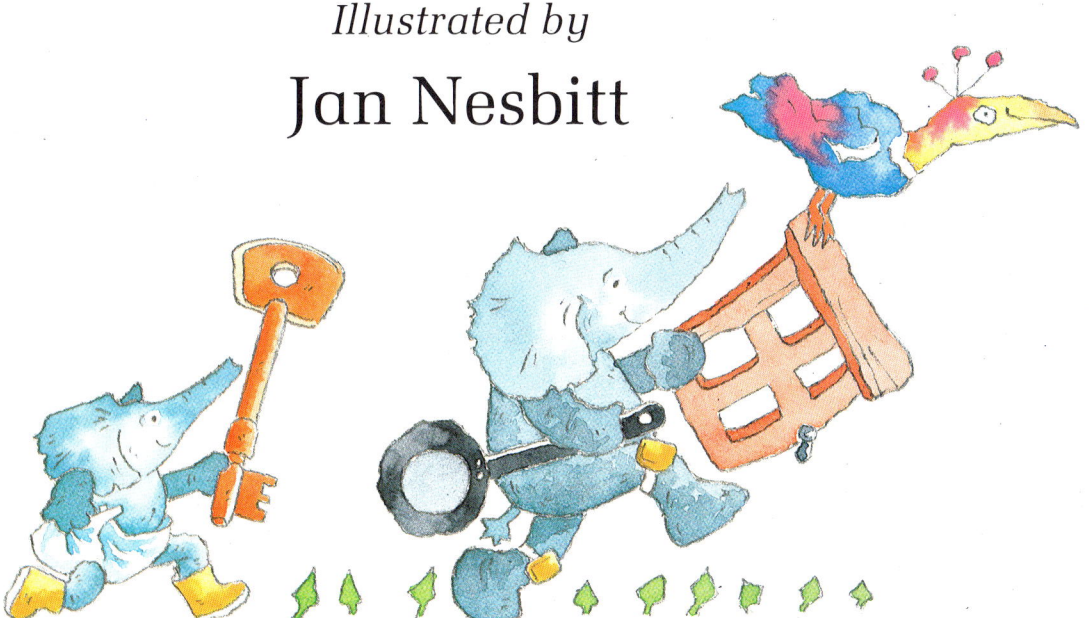

The elephant family have come home from their holiday.

"Oh no!" cries Mum. "Look at our house!"

What has happened?
What will the elephants need to do?

What could they use to build a new house? This picture may give you some ideas.

Draw your new house for the elephants, made out of things you would use.

Mr and Mrs Tusker and their children are making a tent to live in until they get their new house.

Could you design a tent for the elephants?

Make a small pretend tent. You could use sticks, strong glue and fabric.

4

see page C

Rosa and Henry are testing materials to find out which ones will keep the rain out of their tent.

Try doing the test for yourself. Fix materials over some jam jars with elastic bands. Slowly pour a cupful of water onto each material. Which materials would make a good tent?

Where do you think the elephants should choose as a place for their new house?

Where would you build a house for yourself?

Would this be a safe place?

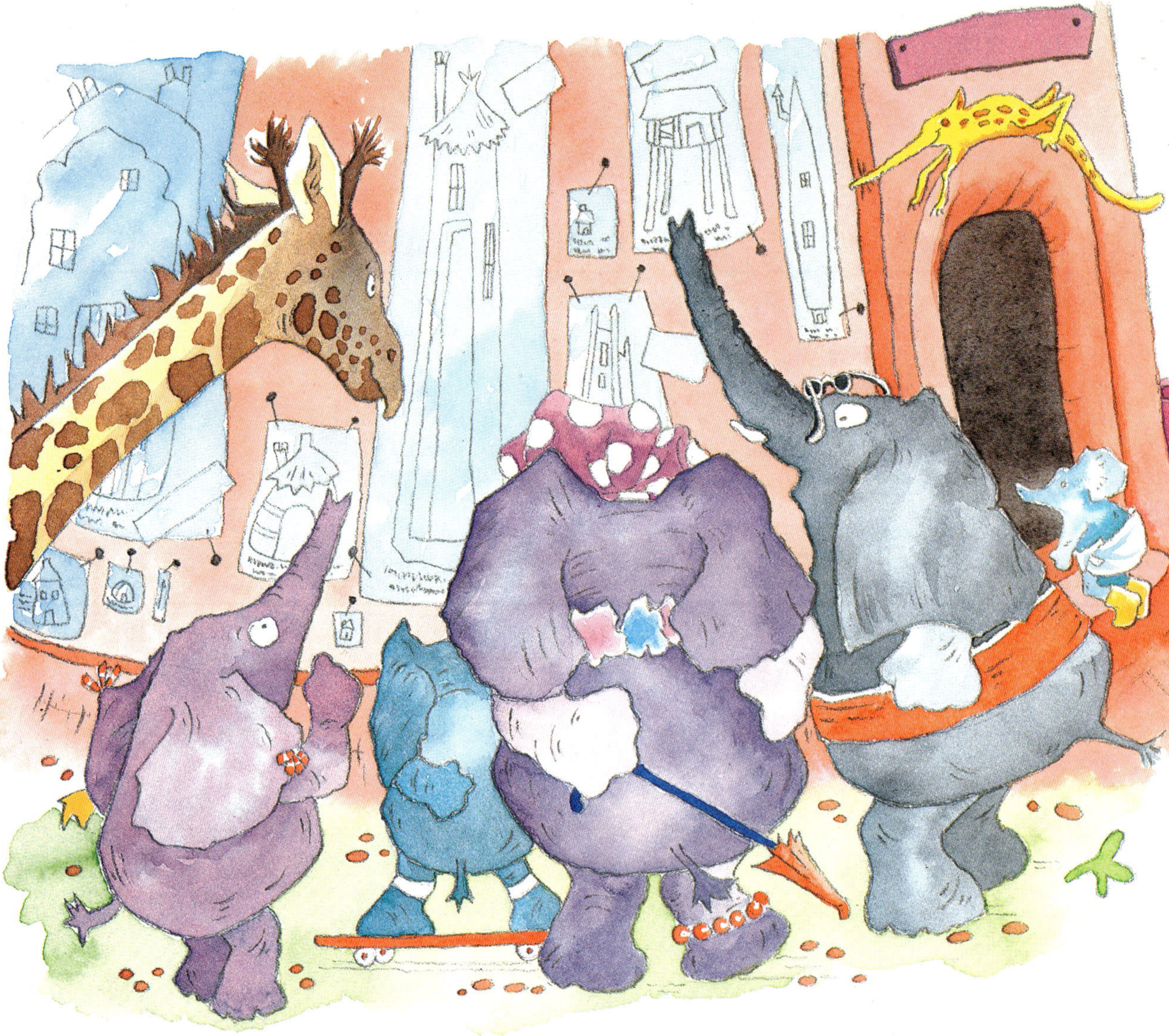

What kind of house do you think they are looking for?

Write about the house they might like. Write about its size and its rooms.

Make a 'House For Sale' poster.

Paint a picture of the house and put your description under it.

see page D

Make a plan of a house for elephants. Draw rooms of different sizes. Say what the rooms are for.

Rosa and Henry have been watching the builder at work on their new house. They wonder what it will look like when it is finished so they are making it with a cardboard box.

Could you make one too? Stick cardboard triangles onto each end of the box for the roof to rest on.

Cut out or paint on windows and doors.

This is great!

The elephant children are making a sign for the gate of their new house.

Why don't you try making a sign for them?

Draw the number onto a piece of card and stick on things like shells or pasta or twigs to decorate it.

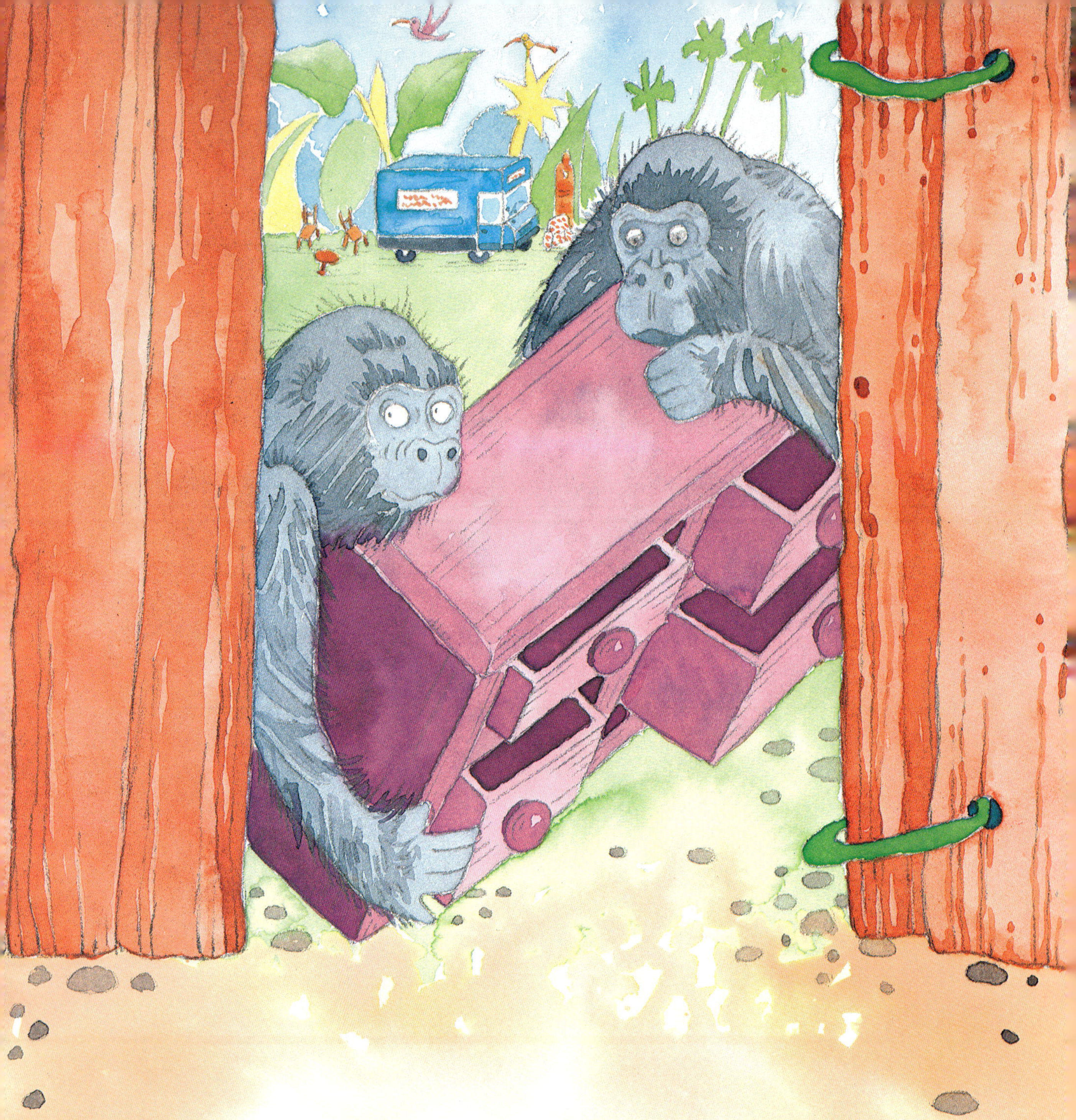

The cupboard won't go through the gap.
How do you think they will solve
the problem?
Is there more than one answer?

Rosa and Henry are making a removal van from a small cardboard box and Lego.
You can make one like this.

Can you think of another way to make a removal van?

see page E

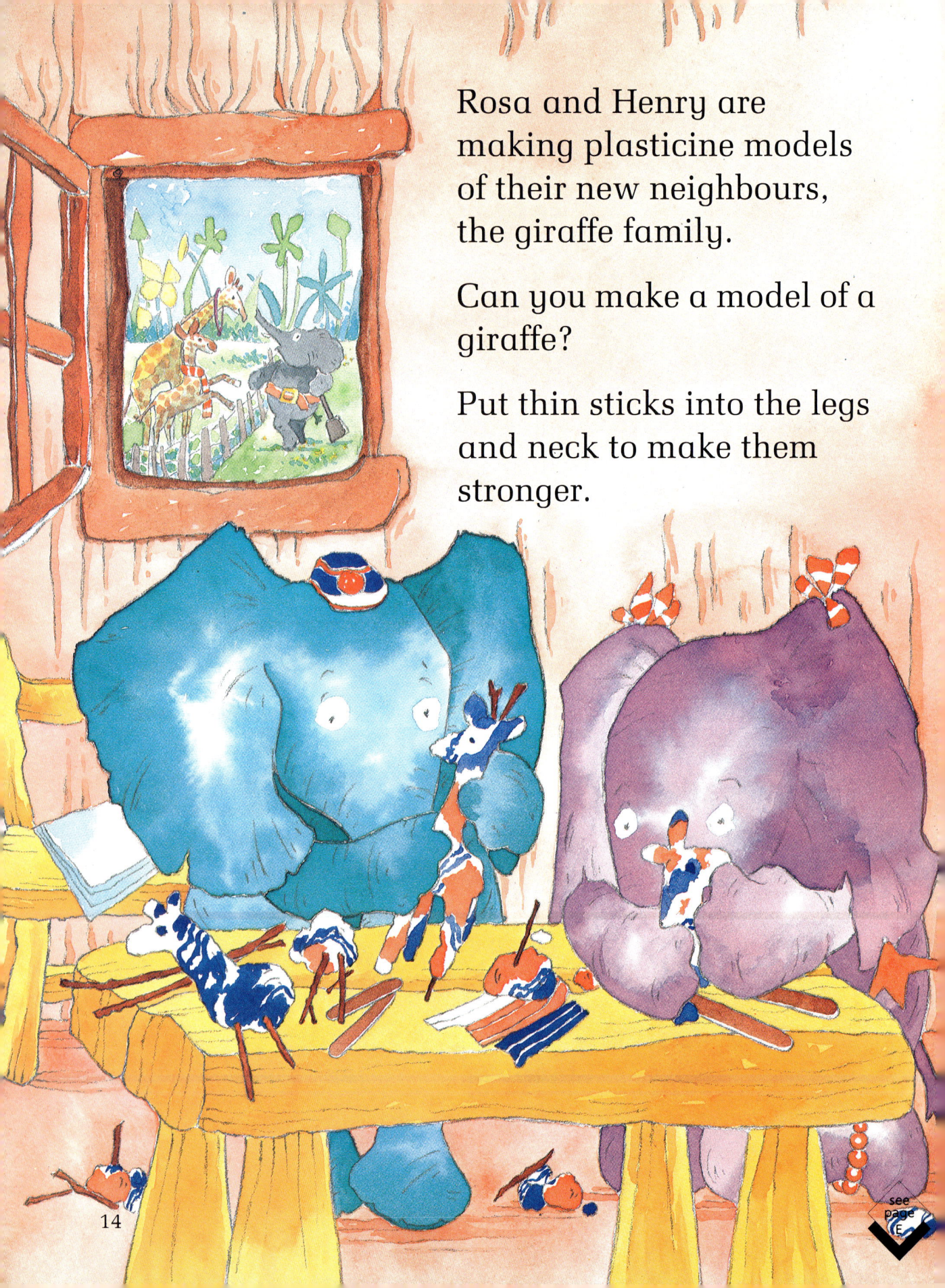

Rosa and Henry are making plasticine models of their new neighbours, the giraffe family.

Can you make a model of a giraffe?

Put thin sticks into the legs and neck to make them stronger.

Look at a pair of scissors. They work in the same way as shears.

What are they made of?

How many pieces are they made from?

You can make a pretend pair of scissors by tracing this shape.

Make 2 pieces the same.

Make a hole where the dot is.

Push a paper fastener through.

PARENTS' GUIDE

The new house

Technology 5 to 6 years

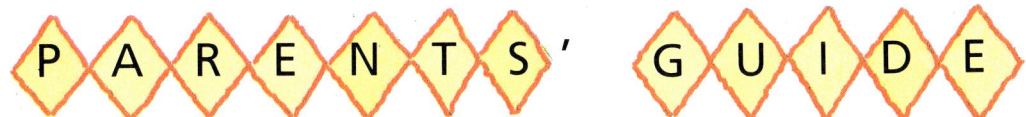

Dear Parent,

The New House covers many skills and concepts that are developed within the National Curriculum programmes of study and attainment targets for Technology with Design.

Technology is concerned with promoting the child's ability to respond to human needs and to encourage independence and self-reliance. He/she must learn to recognise and describe accurately the *need* or opportunity for a design and technology activity. The child must then develop a design to meet the need, using a variety of materials and simple tools. When the work is completed, it must be *evaluated*, recognising what was good and what could be improved or developed further.

The New House focusses on the home and is based on situations which your child will find familiar. It provides a wide range of ideas, all of which are designed to promote technological activity.

Technology links naturally with many other areas of the curriculum and cannot be worked at in isolation. There are therefore a great variety of activities involved in the book. The child will draw pictures, make plans, make models using a variety of media, do simple experiments and find out information. These tasks will help your child to develop an increasingly critical awareness of his or her surroundings.

However there may be a need to extend the activities provided in the book. Your child may be absorbed or interested in a particular area, and might like to work at this further; or he/she may have had difficulties which other activities of a similar nature might help to overcome. To meet these needs, this pull out section provides further activities and opportunities for extending the areas already introduced in the child's book.

A

Helping your child to learn

The activities provided in this book should be enjoyed. Allow your child enough time to get involved, but don't pressure him/her to continue once interest starts to wane. It is better to return to the activity fresh at a later time. Pressure and impatience from parents can kill the interest and enthusiasm which are at the heart of all successful learning.

As far as possible, everything should be done by children themselves, and adults should resist the temptation to take over the activity. It is important that models, pictures, plans and ideas are your child's own work. However your child will, from time to time, need your support, advice and encouragement. He/she will need a receptive adult to talk to about present ideas and future plans.

Materials

It would be helpful if you had some basic equipment readily available and a store of useful odds-and-ends to dip into. Below is a list of some of the items you might like to have in stock or be collecting over a period of time.

scissors • pencils • crayons • felt-tip pens • rubber • ruler • PVA glue • all-purpose clear adhesive • paper • paints • Sellotape • stapler • plasticine or Playdough • small boxes • shoe boxes • Lego or other construction toy • fabric scraps • elastic bands • split pins • pasta shapes • old birthday cards
Stiff cardboard can be cut from large boxes obtained from the supermarket.
Clay – you can now get clay that hardens at room temperature and that can be painted.
Natural objects such as acorns, conkers, pebbles, shells, twigs, leaves, bark, seeds.

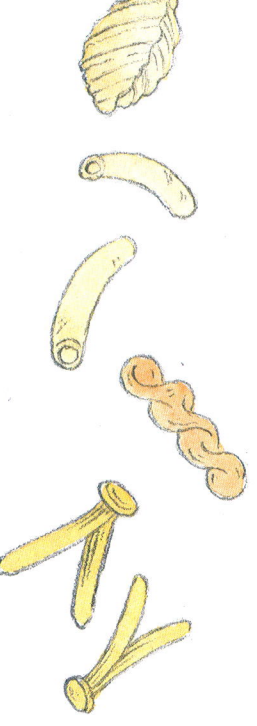

Pages 2 and 3

At this stage it might be worth visiting the zoo and looking at the various types of housing for the different animals. You could draw your child's attention to the great variety of homes provided, from the tall house of the giraffe to the cave-type dens of the bears. Your child could record, in *pictures*, the different types of homes catering for the very different needs of the various animals.

Pages 4 and 5

The frame of the tent can be made by gluing two triangles of sticks and joining them together with further sticks like this, using strong glue. A wigwam type structure is also a possibility with sticks tied at the top.

Having investigated the waterproof properties of different fabrics, the child could *use* this knowledge to think about objects that need to be made out of waterproof materials. He/she could then design and make one of these, e.g. a shopping bag or a rain hat.

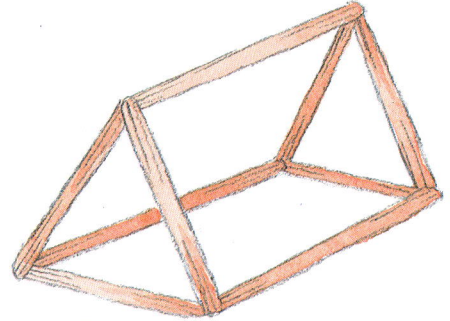

Pages 6 and 7

Talking with your child about the map and listening to his/her ideas will help to develop your child's observation. If the child seems interested in maps, you could help to make a 'map' board game consisting of a track running through a jungle scene, with penalty squares on the route; e.g. poisonous snakes, go back 3. You may have to do the writing, but the ideas and illustrations should be the child's.

Page 8

Your child could make a poster for a pets' home to go into a pet shop window. The format would be the same as for the house poster, e.g. a picture of a mouse cage at the top of the page and a description underneath it.

Page 9

If your child found this activity difficult, he/she could instead draw a large house outline, divide it into upstairs and downstairs and then subdivide areas into 'rooms', which are then labelled. He/she could then plan a home for living in, deciding which rooms to include and which to leave out.

Page 10

If your child enjoyed this activity he/she could go on to design a building with a different purpose, e.g. a factory, a hotel, or a block of flats.

Page 11

Using pictures to represent ideas, your child could think up different jungle signs like
    "BEWARE ELEPHANTS CROSSING"
    "LOW FLYING FLAMINGOES"
    "VICIOUS HISSING SNAKES"
You could look at house signs in your area and your child could make up one to suit your own house, or make a sign for the bedroom door, e.g. BEN'S ROOM. He/she could use seeds, lentils and beans to decorate it.

Page 12

If your child cannot think of a solution you could suggest the following:
a) Could the furniture be got into the house another way, e.g. window?
b) Could it be taken to pieces?
c) As a last resort, could it be sold and a smaller piece bought?

Page 13

Your child could design a logo for the side of the removal van. Questions you could ask are:
"Would a picture on the side of the van help people to recognise it?"
"Which colours would be most eye-catching?"
When out and about on the road you could encourage your child to observe logo designs on vans and lorries.

Page 14

Clay or plasticine modelling will give your child an idea of the limitations of the media as regards its strength, e.g. when constructing long thin legs.

Other animals could be modelled and, when necessary, a stick can be used to strengthen any weak part.

Page 15

You and your child could look together at several tools that work on the same principle as scissors; e.g. pincers and pliers, and garden shears of various types. This activity would need to be supervised and the dangers pointed out to the child.

Pages 16 and 17

This activity takes the child from a plan through to a finished product. This would be a good opportunity to discuss whether the end result was as the child had hoped it would be, or if they would like to change it. If they enjoyed the activity or if they need more practice, they could make a *list* of features they would like in the local park or in the school playground, and then make a *plan* of one of these. It may be to hard to turn this into a model, but it could be turned easily into a picture afterwards.

Pages 18 and 19

When making the climbing frame, an adult will need to cut the potato pieces in advance. Your child will need to press the sticks in quite hard to make them stay. If you own a commercial set of plastic straws and connectors, this will be easier to use.

Page 20

Most probably your child will draw a scarecrow of some kind, but he/she may decide to scare the birds with something that makes a noise, for example. Other ideas are just as valid and could be made and tried out in your own, or in a friend's, garden. If space is limited, you may not want to make a full-size model. For small scarecrow models, rolled-up newpapers make a good base and old tights stuffed with paper will do for a head. Clothing can then be made out of old scraps of fabric. For a full-size scarecrow, sticks and old clothes stuffed with paper look very effective. If your child thinks of a good idea, but it is something that is too hard to make, let him/her *talk* about it, and perhaps even *draw* it.

Pages 22 and 23

Making patterns links well with Art and Craft activites. To help think of a design, the child needs to think about *who* the material is for. Having completed the activity he/she could go on to design patterns for other people or other rooms.
What pattern would a boy like in his room?
What material would look best in the bathroom?
What colours would be best for a baby's room?

Arranging furniture to fit a room is a task that adults frequently do. If you have a dolls' house, your child could be encouraged to rearrange the furniture when playing, if this is not done naturally already.

Over a period of time, your child could make models of several different rooms, which could be as simple or complex as the child's interest and ability allows. The rooms could be decorated with hand-painted wallpaper. There could be a window that opens, and also a door. The furniture could be made out of small boxes, as well as out of Playdough or plasticine.

F

Pages 24 and 25

Sequencing is an activity some children need lots of practice at before they can do it successfully. If your child chooses a well-known story, it will be easier to see how they are managing, though they may well wish to make up their own story for the television programme. It may be easier to make the story first and then make the television to fit the pictures. The local supermarket is a good source of large boxes and the shoe shop has strong, smaller boxes which they are usually happy to give away. This activity can be repeated many times and the programmes can become more complex as the child matures.

Page 26

Home-made cards are a perfect opportunity for practical design in a real situation. The child could be encouraged to make his/her own Christmas and birthday cards. Invitations could be designed and printed out on a photocopier. The design of the invitation could reflect the occasion: e.g. Halloween party cards could be made on witches hat-shaped cards; Firework party invitations could be on rocket-shaped cards. If your child has problems with writing, he/she could dictate what is wanted on the card and you could write it.

Page 27

Other items could be decorated as presents. Strong boxes, once decorated, could make either gift containers or attractive storage boxes. Tins also could be turned into decorative storage containers, provided that there are no longer any sharp edges remaining. They could be painted and then covered with seeds, pasta, shells, fabric, from pictures, from magazines and cards, or from any combination of these.

Pages 28–29

Paper can be decorated in more than one way. Your child could make a string block. You need a block of wood approximately 5cm x 10cm x 2 cm. Pieces of string can be stuck onto the block using a non-water soluble glue. The pattern will vary according to how the string is placed. Some ideas are shown below. The block is then painted and printed in the same way as the vegetables.

  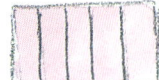 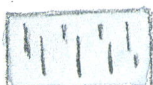 

Pages 30 and 31

The child could be encouraged to make other hats for use in imaginative play. If he/she *draws* the hat first it will give a better idea of what the child wants to make. The ideas may be more ambitious than the child is capable of making on his or her own, and then you will need to step in and help. Hats with a full or partial brim are common requests. This can be achieved by drawing round the base of the main hat onto a piece of card. Draw on an extra piece which will glue inside the main hat shape. Cut it out and snip notches all along the extra drawn piece. Bend the notched pieces up and glue inside the hat.

Page 32

A variety of solutions are possible. If your child needs help, suggest he or she finds out how other people stop doors banging. Encourage children to talk about their ideas.

A large stone, perhaps obtained on a beach holiday, could be painted and then varnished. Clay could be turned into any model, provided it is fairly compact and doesn't have too many fine details that might chip off. Material could be made into a padded shape and hung over the door handles to pad the door, should it try to bang shut.

What do you have to play with in your garden?

Which apparatus do you like best? Why?

Draw a picture of an exciting new playground.

Dad will make Rosa and Henry a climbing frame, if they draw him what they want.

Draw what you think it will look like.

You can make your design with cocktail sticks and cubes of potato.

Mr Tusker is going to need a bird scarer.

What do gardeners and farmers use to scare birds?

Draw your idea for a bird scarer. Can you make your idea?

You can make a garden of your own.
Here are some things you could use.

1 gravel
2 compost
3 moss grass
4 mirror pond
5 twigs trees
6 box shed
7 stones path
8 paper and plasticine flowers

The furniture in Rosa's bedroom needs to be arranged so that Henry doesn't upset things every time he comes in.

There are no covers on the beds yet. Henry and Rosa can't decide what patterns to have?

Make a pattern using paints or crayons that they would like for curtains and bed covers.

Make a bedroom with a box and furniture with plasticine and you can try arranging the furniture.

Henry and Rosa think the television is boring. They think they could make a better programme themselves. They start by making the television.

Rosa thinks of a good story.
She gets lots of paper and makes a different picture on each sheet.
She puts them in order and Sellotapes them together.

They put the end through the television picture slots and pull the pictures through.

Make a television and programme like Henry and Rosa. You could show it to your family and friends.

Rosa and Henry are posting invitations to their house warming party.

Could you make an invitation card? You could make it an interesting shape.

What information needs to go on it? You could look at other cards to find out.

Will I get one?

"They'll never guess!"

Can you guess what the presents are from their shapes?

Play a guessing game with your family and friends.

Wrap up different shaped things in paper. Can anyone guess what they are?

see page G

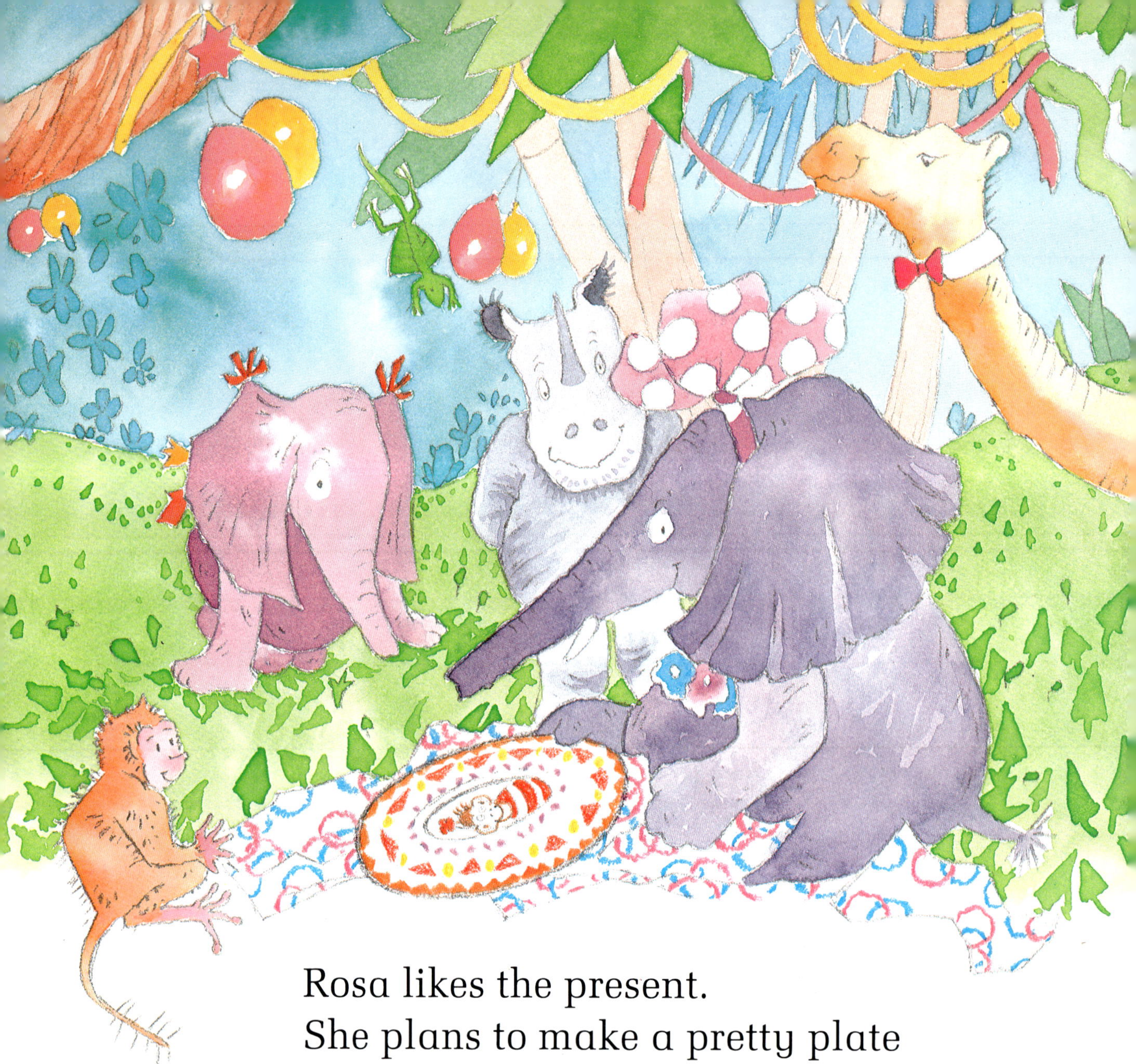

Rosa likes the present.
She plans to make a pretty plate
for her room tomorrow.

If you had a paper plate and
felt-tip pens, could you do the
same as Rosa?

You could try out your ideas on
paper first.

see page H

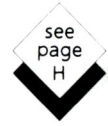

The Rhinos made their own wrapping paper for their presents.
They used vegetables cut in half to print patterns.

They paint half a cut vegetable and press it onto paper lots of times.

Try making your own wrapping paper.

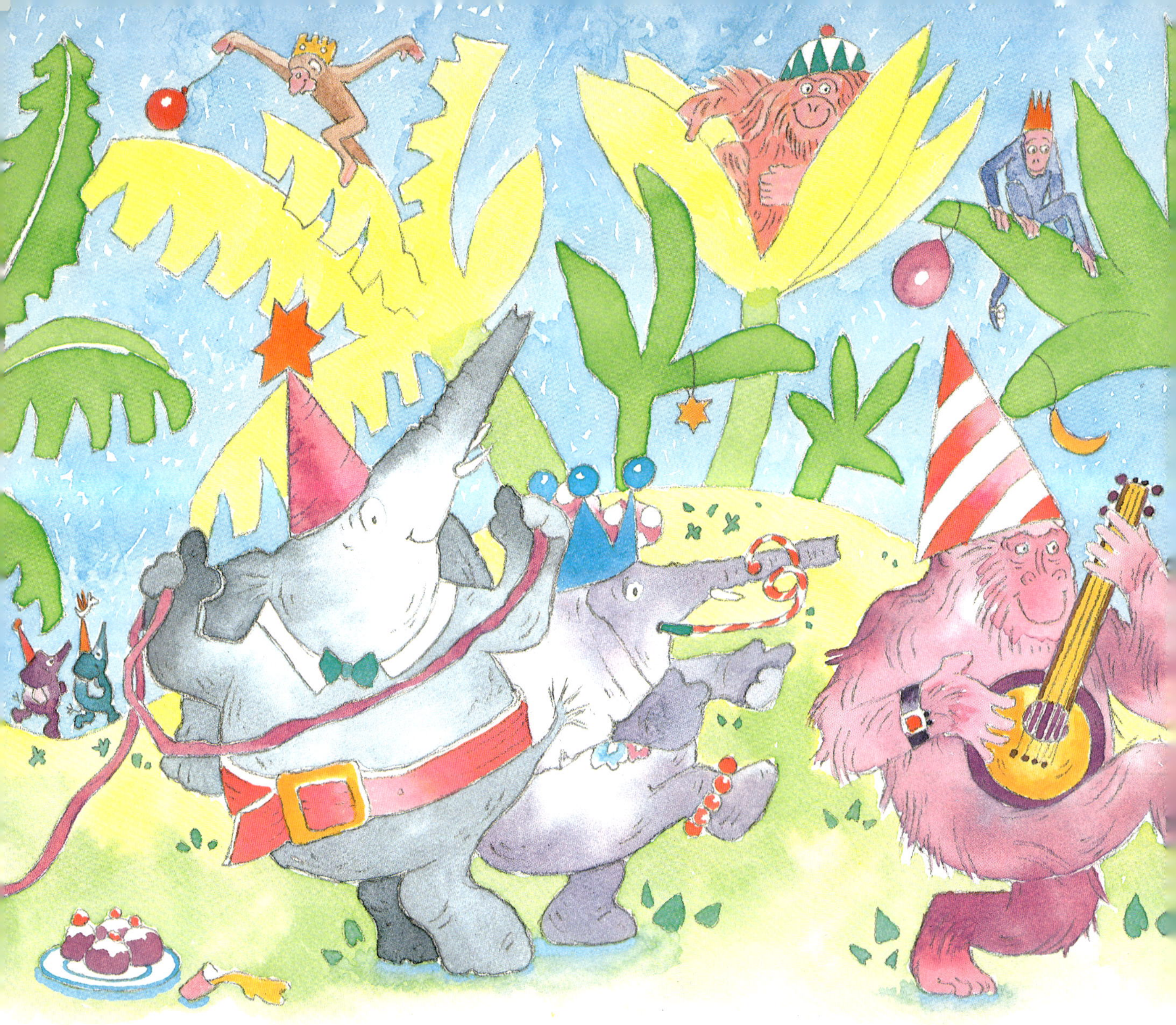

If you were going to the party
what sort of hat would you wear?

Could you make your own?

Start with a strip of card.
Fix it round your head.
Sellotape the ends together.

Round this you can glue paper and cut fancy shapes.

You can add card pictures that stick up.

You could add coloured paper and fringes to decorate it.

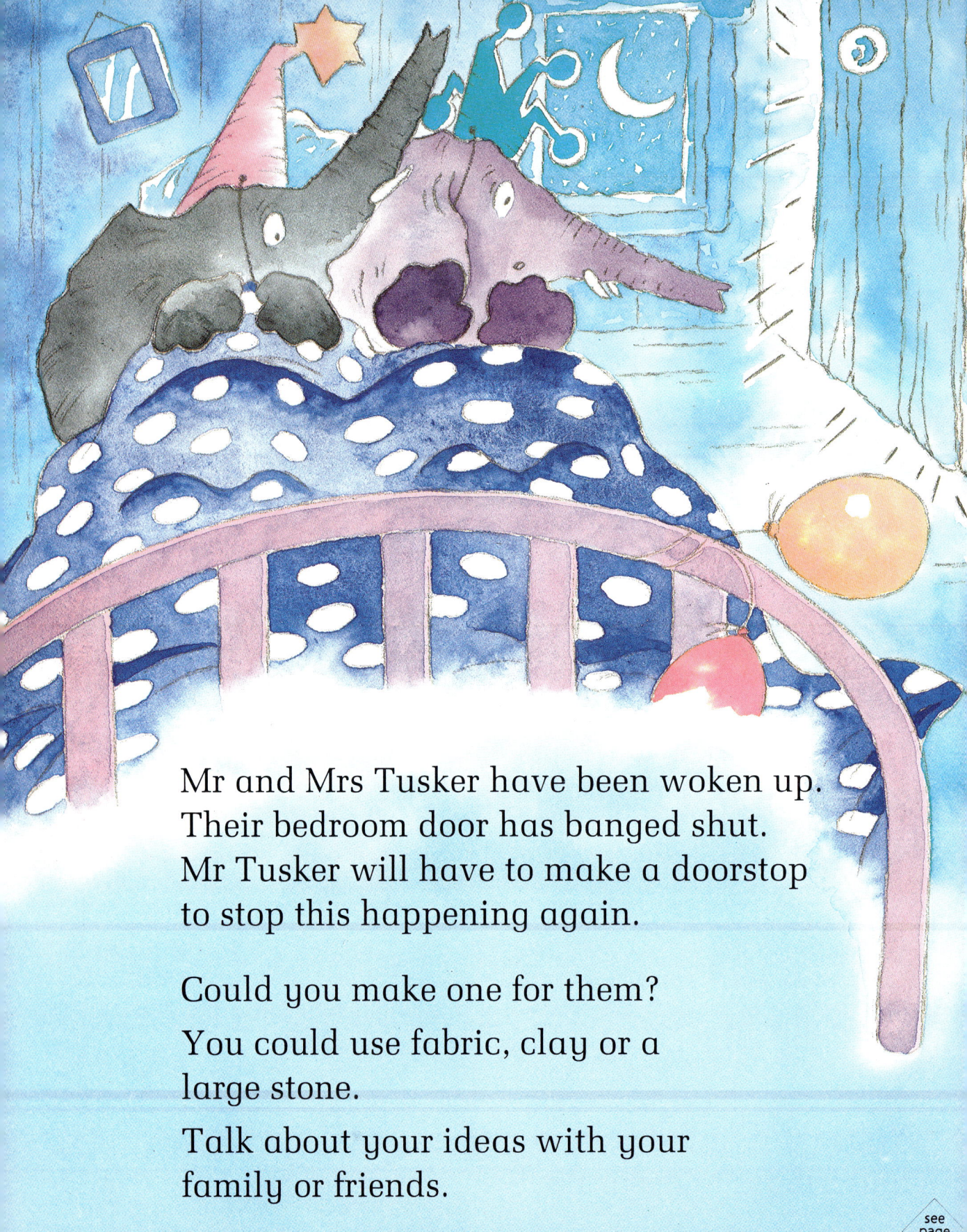

Mr and Mrs Tusker have been woken up. Their bedroom door has banged shut. Mr Tusker will have to make a doorstop to stop this happening again.

Could you make one for them?

You could use fabric, clay or a large stone.

Talk about your ideas with your family or friends.

see page H